Heavenly

Inspirations

Manifested

Published by Advantage, Charleston, South Carolina.
Member of Advantage Media Group.

ADVANTAGE is a registered trademark and the Advantage colophon is a trademark of Advantage Media Group, Inc.

Printed in the United States of America.

ISBN: 978-1-59932-050-2

Most Advantage Media Group titles are available at special quantity discounts for bulk purchases for sales promotions, premiums, fundraising, and educational use. Special versions or book excerpts can also be created to fit specific needs.

For more information, please write: Special Markets, Advantage Media Group, P.O. Box 272, Charleston, SC 29402 or call 1.866.775.1696.

HEAVENLY
INSPIRATIONS
MANIFESTED

A Poetic Expression of Life

By TRACEE Y. WELLS, *Professional Life Coach*

Dedication

I most graciously and reverently, dedicate this collection of poems to God, the Father, His Son, Jesus and the precious Holy Spirit. Without His love, grace and faithfulness, this book would be just a sweet spiritual dream and would have never become a manifested reality.

Most importantly, I would like to thank God for the gift of poetry. This gift is His way of loving the world through me. I pray the content of this book will inspire God's people to maintain an intimate and steadfast relationship with Christ in facing all seasons of life.

From my teen-aged years until now, I have always loved and enjoyed writing. I was inspired by my father, the late Newty W. Moreland at a very early age to write poetry. Daddy never completed one manuscript and even had many of his works stolen. His life was forfeited so prematurely at the age of fifty years old. Vivid memories of him reciting his inspirational work now flood my soul, as I recall his dying bedside request to never let my dreams die. Although I may never retrieve much of his life's work, as the reel-to-reel tapes of the Seventies have been damaged or destroyed. I was able to discover two of his greatest poetic writings in a dirty, old basement chest. I believe God is still honoring him in his death over two decades later. Our faithful God has allowed and granted me the very special privilege of including them in my compilation of poems. Somehow I believe God will let him know they have been published, and I know he will be proud of my pursuit to live my dreams. I salute and pay tribute to you Dad, one of the greatest unknown poets the world will only hear and taste a glimpse of. Your legacy will continually live through me and in the heart of my writing forever.

My mother, Eloise Moreland-Dunham is truly a praying woman of God who pushed me endlessly during the birthing process of this book; she was one relentless Lamaze partner! Not a single day went by that did not echo her encouraging words to me. She would say, "Keep on writing, stay focused, and quit being slothful." Months prior to the completion of my manuscript, I will never forget her mini sermon on the sluggard and the unparalleled diligence of the ant spoken of in Proverbs 6: 6-11. Thanks, Mom! You have witnessed my life from a front row seat and observed my sowing through many tears. Praise be to God, who has graced you to live and see the reaping of His great joy in my life. I could never have done it without you!

And what can I say about my man child from above, my son Caleb. You have been such a joy and inspiration. As I look over the years, I realize that you were raising me just as much as I was raising you. What lessons and depth God has shown me of His everlasting love for His children through your eyes!

I attribute my ability to keep my head high and my heart humble to my dear grandmother, Louisa Moreland-Flute and late grandfather, Newton Webster Moreland who were both integral links and the family guides to salvation. They taught our family about true wholesome, honest Christian living and were strong spiritual pillars for many decades. Grandmother made it her life's mission to evangelize the world around her. She provided fundamental Christian education to all whom she touched, and even directed bible school and camp during the summer months for family members and many church and neighborhood children. Her daily curriculum included not only bible study, but French, typing, piano and vocal lessons, with a summer's end open recital. She is and will always be "Grandma" to literally hundreds upon hundreds of children and families.

I also extend a special dedication to my step-parents. The late Robert L. Dunham totally broke the mold as it relates to the "Ultimate Step-

Dad". He understood the art of effective co-parenting and did a most wonderful job, leaving an example to be modeled by blended families for a lifetime. Nellie Washington, my step-mother and a very gifted pianist, is also a woman of many who contributed to my concept of young womanhood and strengthened my love and passion for music. Thanks a million. I'll never forget the countless hours of practicing on that black baby grand piano!

I could not stop without mentioning the continual and unconditional love, support and endless counsel of my precious brothers and sister, DeNewt, Mike, Jeff, Keishan and a loving family and community of in-laws, uncles, aunts, nephews, nieces, cousins, adopted family and special friends. I know how tremendously blessed I am to have so many people share such a significant part of my life.

Lastly, I want to sincerely honor and salute a host of spiritual parents including my Pastor and State Bishop, Freddie L. Brown, Jr. and the New Jerusalem Full Gospel Baptist Church family in Portland, OR, Apostle Lafayette Scales of Rhema Christian Center in Columbus, OH, Co-Pastor Marva Mitchell and the late Bishop Willie E. Mitchell of Revival Center Ministries International in Dayton, OH, and the Reverend P.E. Henderson, Jr., the late Reverend P.E. and Aquilla Henderson, Sr. of the Corinthian Baptist Church in Dayton, OH where I attended as a child. With God as my Rock, these very special people have aided in my establishing a firm spiritual foundation. These true spiritual leaders and forerunners have dramatically touched my life, and have greatly guided and enhanced my development in this Great Gospel of Jesus Christ.

I love you all from the bottom of my heart!

In God's Love Always,
Tracee

Contents

"Faithful as He"

"That Sinful Estate"

"Anchored in the Light"

"Dark Shadows" (Author: *"Daddy"*, the late Newty W. Moreland)

"Stranger Named Loved" (Author: the late Newty W. Moreland)

"Going Home" (Dedication: the late Marshall Flute)

"They're Coming In"

"Thanks, God"

"The Bow and Arrows of Hate"

"Forever and Always Friends" (Dedication: Melissa Redman)

" Friendship" (Dedication: Tracy Fletcher & Sandy Sanders)

"Steadfast Awhile" (Dedication: *"Sister"*, Keishan Dorsey)

"Just Like the Eagle" (Dedication: *"Moma"*, Eloise Moreland-Dunham)

" Daughter of Jerusalem" (Dedication: Cindy Simmons)

"I'm Depending on You"

"Whom Shall I Fear?"

"Jesus Lord, Our Redeemer"

"A Grandmother" (Dedication: *"Granny"*, Louisa Moreland-Flute)

"A Great Day"

"Ropes of Iron"

"Who Am I?" (Dedication: *"Nephew"*, Webster *"Webbie"* Moreland)

"Give Unto the Lord"

"Too Much is Given"

"Heaven Awaits"

"To Be Called a Servant" (Dedication: The Corporate Leadership & Body of Christ)

"All Answers He Knows"

"Glad to Be Me"

"My Greatest Love Story"

"Will You Receive Him?"

"Still Much Work to Be Done"

"The Love of Jesus"

"My Savior Lives"

"A Greater Glory" (Dedication: the late Bishop Willie E. Mitchell)

"Holy World Without End"

"O, Worthy Potter"

"I Will Arise"

"Sisterhood in Christ" (Dedication: Daphne Harris)

"The Old Folks Use to Say" (the late Paul Lawrence Dunbar)

"Time Verses Sloth"

Love & Marriage - 83
PRELUDE TO LOVE

"Take My Hand & Share in My World"

"Together in Love"

"Forever Keepsake"

"Husbands & Wives"

"I'll Always Love You"

"In God Lies Our Strength"

"Will You Still"

"Marriage: Be Willing to Wait"

"Your Love for Me"

"True Love"

Preface

The poetry of *Heavenly Inspirations Manifested (HIM)* emphasizes the love and faithfulness of God's unchanging hand in my personal life and in the lives of His children alike. These writings serve as my personal set of psalms and have been written over the span of twenty years. They express unspeakable joy and peace during mountain-top victories and triumphs, yet they also express hope and encouragement when facing the trials and testing found in the daily circumstances of our lives.

Reflecting upon the divine balances of life and even nature itself, this work seeks to fervently drive the heart of mankind to receive the eternal gift of salvation. Salvation is offered solely through God's redemptive plan in Christ Jesus. It is a gift that has been divinely purchased and freely offered to everyone (Rom. 10:8-13).

One may even find a present life scenario in the core of the pieces contained in this book. It is my prayer that the sharing of this expressive work will evoke a proper and rapid response to God and His Word, both individually and corporately.

I challenge you, the reader, to pursue the wholesome course of Christ. It is a course that entails both His glory and sufferings. In receiving this blessed invitation, you will fully develop a holy and loving relationship with Jesus and begin to experience the abundant life He offers us all on Earth and in the eternal life to come in Heaven.

Introduction

The Lord has given me the mandate to write and release this collection of poems to show forth the wondrous love, righteousness, peace and joy of the kingdom of God. The title of this book, *Heavenly Inspirations Manifested (HIM)*, makes reference to the reality of Heaven and our belonging to the celestial realm, our true state of existence. These poetic inspirations have been disclosed from the privy chamber of God through the sum of my life experiences. They have not come by the will of man, but have been God-breathed and inspired. In essence, I speak of the things which I have made touching the King; therefore, my tongue is the pen of a ready writer (II Peter 1:21 & Ps. 45:1).

The world stands in the dire need of a practical and manifested revelation of truth to inspire the need for salvation, maturity in God, and the exhortation of holy and righteous living, especially in the face of opposition. Our very life force rests in God who so seeks to freely give to His beloved the greatest source and resource that has and will ever be known to mankind and creation; the precious and very life of His dear Son, Jesus the Christ.

The *manifestation of truth* is to exhibit, express, or make known the application of truth. It literally refers to actual conception or the "*giving of birth*" to truth. God, the Father through the person of Jesus did just that! He was manifested and "birthed" in the flesh (Jn. 1:14), and only the spiritual rebirth of mankind will produce a right standing with God. Jesus then has the capacity to manifest or birth truth in our personal lives, while miraculously commending our conscience in the sight of God (II Cor. 4:2 & Heb. 9:14).

Oh, to see the manifestation of the sons of God! This is the earnest expectation of the creature and the whole creation, which groaneth and travaileth together until now. All await the adoption to wit the redemption of the body (Rom. 8:19-23).

We must inevitably conclude, the world at large beckons for the divine conception and "birth of truth". Mankind is hungry for the covenant and eternal establishment of truth on Earth as it has been eternally established in Heaven.

It is the sincere desire of God to utilize this book and the vessel of sacred poetry as an open door of utterance to reveal the great and wonderful mysteries of the Gospel (Eph. 6:19-20 & Col. 4:3-4).

This is the prophetic hour, when we must move as the corporate Body of Christ from revelation, inspiration to **the power of MANIFESTATION!**

Soliloquies of Life

THE HISTORY OF SOLILOQUY

Soliloquy was birthed in Western drama during the Medieval and Renaissance period. They are since known as "*monologues*," wherein a single character or actor speaks alone through reflective utterance, declaration or poetic expression. Although the conventions of soliloquy of that day were restricted by the speech of characters, playwrights such as Shakespeare exercised a new freedom of thought and brought great creativity to standard conventions during the late 16th and early 17th century in plays such as "Hamlet" and its well known soliloquy, "*To be or not to be.*" Many critics and scholars debate on whether the history of soliloquy was intended to be "*self addressed*", "*audience addressed*" or an "*alternating combination*" of both speeches.

I choose not to be part of the critical debate, but view the drama of soliloquy as any other art form in history, which should be coupled with the personal freedom to transcend and transform in and through the mind of the artist.

As I think and meditate on the Book of Psalms, written primarily by King David, they are real life accounts of declarations, confessions, songs and poetic writings indicative of his life journey as a leader, warrior, fugitive, sacred musician to ultimately one of the greatest reigning Kings in the history of Israel (I Sam.16:1-13). Although David expresses his hope and confidence in God through praise, worship and poetry, he also makes confessions to God of his human infirmities and personal sin, raging internal battles, distressful circumstances, numerous disappointments and what he often perceived as insurmountable fears.

These heavenly writings and inspirations are significantly marked with his most personal and deepest meditations and self-evaluations, through song, prayer, conversation *and* monologue addressed to himself *and* to his divine Creator. However, many Christians and readers today receive the advantage and draw from the benefit of his written life examples and touch of soliloquy in his writings. His soul reflection and heart's cry has given millions an anchor of hope, supernatural courage, renewed faith and strength during some of the most God-confident and desperate hours in their lives. Readers and audiences all over the world are continually moved, challenged and transformed by its pages.

In essence, the Book of Psalms and the divine Scriptures on a whole, known as the "*Holy Bible*" is still the best selling book of all time and has the most popular and panoramic audience that ever has and will exist.

"THIS PEN"

I love to write; it frees my mind.
This pen expresses my imagination.
It vents my thoughts, attitude, and mood,
And helps to relieve my frustrations.

This pen is a channel my gift flows through.
I know that this was sent from above,
To share with the world an inspiring word;
For this is God's gift of love.

There, too, is a gift and a talent that lies,
Awaiting in the heart of each soul.
Only you can seize it, search it out,
And give it the room to grow.

My heart is happy, my soul is free
So much joy in my innermost man;
When I think on the goodness, the gift that God gave,
And His love shown through this pen.

PASSION VERSE: PS. 45:1

"MY ROCK"

He's my Rock when the billows roll.
What a dear friend of mine.
Peace in spirit and understanding
In His comfort I always find.

My trumpet starting each day off
To a glorious and winning start.
The only true Rock and motivation
That anchors within my heart.

There is never a passing day,
That He fails to rescue me,
From the flaws of my own character,
Sending my soul bound-free.

_R_ is for His righteousness,
That is every holy and true.
_O_ outlines His mighty strength
That helps mankind to endure.
_C_ carves the rugged cross,
And the sacrificing of His blood.
_K_ kindles the spiritual hope
And salvation given through His love.

So, never fret; no neither fear
Any hour upon the clock.
You're no longer a slave to sin and death,
For in Jesus lies your security, your Rock!

PASSION VERSES: II SAM. 22: 2-3; 32-33

"THE ANOINTING OF GOD"

When the anointing of God abides in you....
You can leap the highest mountain,
Swim the seven seas,
Find His fish in deep waters,
And minister to their needs.
When the anointing of God rests upon you....

When the anointing of God abides in you....
You will run and not be weary,
Walk and not faint,
Tackle the invincible,
You're sheltered warm and safe.
When the anointing of God rest upon you....

When the anointing of God abides in you....
You're faith will never fail you,
Hope will never die,
Evidence of the things unseen
Will appear before you're eyes.
When the anointing of God rest upon you....

When the anointing of God abides in you....
Your purpose and destiny unfolds,
Direction is revealed,
Doors begin to open,
He'll even make time stand still.
When the anointing of God rest upon you....

The Answer?
Allow the anointing of God to rest upon you.

PASSION VERSES: I JN. 2: 24, 27

"THE BEGINNING"

Behind every mirror, there stands a man,
Made in the holy image of God.
Vessels created from the dust of the ground,
He molded us one by one.

The sweet breath of life did our Father breathe
To declare man a living soul;
Placing beneath his feet dominion and power
Over every creeping thing below.

He imparted to man a spirit, soul and body
To lift praise and bring honor to His name;
An instrument of love; designed to walk holy,
And made in just one day.

I can hear the voice of the Trinity speak,
"It is not good for man to be alone."
So, causing a deep sleep to fall upon man's face,
From his rib He created a new mold.

A help meet was given, and He called her woman,
Yes, she would be the mother of all.
The two were commanded to be fruitful and increase,
And to heed to the righteous call.

The call of instruction, the commandment of God,
To eat of all freely, but one tree.
For the tree that sat in the midst of the garden,
Was there only for them to see.

Not to touch, nor to eat,
For God stated, "Or you will surely die."
Yet deceived by the serpent, Eve ate of the fruit,
As she saw it quite pleasing to the eye.

She gave this fruit to her husband to eat,
As the eyes of both were opened.
Thus, the fall of man reached conception,
Leaving heartache and death as its token.

Yet God already had a master plan,
For He knew in all wisdom man would fail,
Falling short of the very thing He had asked,
Allowing disobedience and sin to prevail.

So, loving the world and the man He created,
God gave the life of His only begotten Son.
And through Jesus, our Lord, the price was paid,
Enabling God and man to atone.

Now reconciled to God, man again stands,
For now he has the true hope of winning.
And we learn today from this historic account,
For it was so... from The Beginning.

PASSION VERSES: GEN. 1: 26-31; 2: 8-
9; 15-25; 3: 4-7 & ROM. 5: 12-15

"THE WORLD, THE WORLD"

The world, the world this place where man abides.
It's colored with sin and slowly it dies.

Practicing so freely every little wicked thing;
Offering mere hopelessness to the songs that I sing.

Its occupants run so wildly and free,
Determined to ruin the life in me.

Its focus holds no honor, guilt or shame;
Seeking only control of a single soul to claim.

But Lord, Jesus you have given the victory to me.
Your banner of truth has surely made me free.

From the rudiments of a land that grew from a lie,
From the world, the wicked world Lord hear my cry!

PASSION VERSES: PS. 34: 15-22; 60:4; 61: 1-4, I JN. 5:4-5 & JN. 16:33

"A TRAVELING MAN"

This house, this home is a corruptible shell
Why does man value it so?
For this vessel is merely a temporary place,
And for awhile it was given to each soul.

I am so glad to say a tomorrow awaits
Where there will be a true place of rest.
Never seen by naked eyes, never touched by mortal hand,
A home with a heavenly address.

Though the walk be long and difficult sometimes,
Its mean grants true holiness and consecration.
For we are considered only a traveling man
In constant journey and seeking holy destination.

PASSION VERSES: JN. 14:1-3, I COR. 15:50-55 & II COR. 5:1-9

"SEEDS OF LIFE"

Seeds of life, seeds of love....
Seeds of hope, seeds of joy....

Seeds of sorrow, guilt and shame....
Seeds of strife, seeds of pain....

To every seed a harvest brings the essence of its rite,
No matter how we pick or choose to plant our seeds in life.

PASSION VERSES: GAL. 6:7-10, PS. 126: 5-
6, PROV. 6: 12-15; 22:8:9 & ROM. 6:19-23

"I SEE GOD"

Some men only look for God high in the sky,
And for the life of me, I don't know why.

For His grace has appeared to each and everyone of us.
I see God in my heart and do wholly trust.

In miracles only do many feel He exist.
Yet I see God in my grandmother's kiss.

I see God in trials as He reaches for my hand,
Also in the joyous times when life appears so grand.

Why solely search for God in the seemingly greater things?
God abides in the smallest tree, and to them He doth cling.

This continual thought ponders my mind while I sleep,
So my friends, wait patiently while it I do repeat.

We only look for God high in the sky,
And for the life of me I don't know why.

PASSION VERSES: MT. 5:8; 13:13-17

"MIGHTY MAN OF GOD"

A mighty man of God, indeed you are.
You may not feel it all the time.
But His gracious love is suffering long
To guide your every stride.

No step you make is not ordained,
While you wonder which way to go.
He will perfect all that concerns you.
Your election sure and true.

Mighty man of God, you're what I see.
It's the omega; yes, it's your end.
As God cares more for the fruit tree itself
Than the apple upon its limb.

And when you begin to see yourself
The way God sees you now,
You will face your fears without a doubt
And wholly honor your covenant vow.

Yes, you are a mighty man of God!

PASSION VERSES: ROM. 8:1-4, JN. 3:20-22, PS.
37: 23-24; 138:8, II PET. 1:3-11 & PHIL. 1:6

"RAINY DAYS"

The sky is bleak, all cloudy and gray.
It looks like it's gonna' be a rainy day.

While the sky lies hidden beyond the dark clouds,
Raindrops feed the earth and become its shroud.

Rainy days are a grim reminder of the rainy days in life.
The blue sky can't be seen, only the heartache of strife.

The air most time is chilly and cool,
And sometimes are attitudes reflect this mood.

Why must there be both sunshine and rain?
I guess it's the balance that God has made.

Would there be an up, if there was never a down?
Could we really smile, if we never frowned?

So, as I pull back the shade and look outside,
I will adjust my hope as it rains this time.

I will appreciate the good times as Heaven opens its gates,
And realize that God has determined my fate.

Yes, the sky is bleak all cloudy and gray,
But though the rain falls, I will rejoice in this day!

PASSION VERSES: I PET. 4: 12-13, PHIL. 4:4 & PS. 33:21

"MOOD SWINGS"

At first you're happy, then you're sad.
One minute you cry, the next you're glad.

You woke up angry, went to bed with fear.
Inside you're hurting, just seeking to live.

Undecided you are, can't make up your mind.
All you're ways are unstable, yet you wonder why.

You want the sweet, but won't let go of the bitter.
Mood Swings…Mood Swings, aren't you tired?

You life is leading to a dead end now,
But you can't face it; you're just too proud!

You've traded your oil and soberness within
To entertain wine and vinegar, my friend.

But it's not over, believe it or not.
You can be set free if you truly want.

The worst enemy is your own human will.
Just yield it to God, and then be still.

Only make the stand and loose this world.
It's not worth the heartache, death and control.

God has given this life for you to live
To shake those Mood Swings sent by sin.

PASSION VERSES: JAS. 1:8; 3:10-18, ROM. 8: 6-13 & I PET. 1:13

"THE HOUR TICKS NIGH"

Dark as the night this world will be;
Darkened in shadows of perpetuity.
When the day disappears, the nightfall will ascend,
Covering all the earth to reckon its end.

Wake up ye nations, light your fires a'flame.
The chariot is coming, and Jesus will reign!

Keep your lamp filled with oil,
And your light a'glow,
For this destined hour, only He knows.

As a thief it will creep
On all those who sleep.
Awake ye Zion!
Arise ye sheep!

Live only to hear to the trumpet cry,
Jesus is coming, He's coming,
For the hour ticks nigh!

PASSION VERSES: MK. 13; MT. 25: 1-13; I
THESS. 4:16-18; 5: 1-10 & REV. 16:15

"MY BABY, BABY"

He knew you in my womb.
My baby, baby not a moment to soon.

Inside me your little life grew.
My baby, baby you're a dream come true.

You man child; yes, mine for awhile.
I'm bubbly within at your beautiful smile.

Great and mighty exploits you will do.
By His great name alone, He has summoned you.

All things you will do in Him,
And His big light will shine before all men.

End time harvest you shall bring in.
My baby, baby… what peace is your end!

PASSION VERSES: JER. 1:5-10; ACTS 2:17-21 & LK. 10:2

"I'VE HEALED YOUR WOUNDED HEART"

I have seen your tears and your many fears,
All of the pain that your life has yielded;
Your childhood scars, your wounded heart,
And your innermost secrets you have hidden.

I have answered your prayers, taken your cares,
And placed you upon this mountain-top.
No man or fame, nor fortune or gain
Has brought you this blessed lot!

I shall keep you from falling, but yet I am calling,
Tugging you to higher worship and praise.
It is I who have healed your wounded heart.
So, be faithful to me always.

PASSION VERSES: PS. 34:17-19; 147: 1,3 & IS. 53: 4-5

"WEEPING MAY ENDURE"

Does it ever seem like the harder you try
Things just seem to get worse?
You put forth much effort to make it better,
But are always the one who gets hurt.

You're tired of pushing, grinning, and bearing it all
Always stuck with the short end of the stick,
Debating from the core of your hurting heart,
If you should go on or quit.

Sometimes we all feel this way,
For life's sorrows are real and true.
But we can't grow weary in doing well,
For God will always come through!

Life is not easy much of the time.
This fellowship must be shared with Christ.
For if we share in His glory, we must share in His pain,
And the carnal must be willing to die.

Remember that the darkest and coldest hour
Is always before a new day of dawning.
Yes, weeping may endure for a night, my child,
But joy shall come in the morning!

PASSION VERSES: I PET. 1: 6-7, PHIL. 3: 10-
11, ROM. 8:16-18, PS. 126: 5-6 & 30:4-5

"THE THRONE ROOM OF GOD"

I had to laugh; I had to smile,
As I looked toward Heaven today.
For the Lord is faithful, and His words are true.
In Him I am blessed always.

The Great I Am; yes, whatever I need
Is found in His mercy seat of grace.
The throne room of God, where the cherubim reside,
I gained access to the holy place.

Running through the veil, my soul fled
To the spiritual part of my man.
Laying hold I anchored my victory assure,
Finding that this was always the plan.

It was there where I made my petitions known,
Standing boldly with the Lamb's blood in my hands.
It was then that I came to fully understand
That this was God's position for man.

Now I'm wholly persuaded, we must press through God's shrine,
Meeting face to face our Holy One.
For the right position for deliverance, victory and grace
Is in the throne room of God!

PASSION VERSES: HEB. 4:14-16; 9: 1-6 & 11-14

"FAITHFUL AS HE"

Forgive me, Dear Lord, for the way is hard,
And I stumble much of the time.
I must learn to seek you with fullness of life,
And allow Your great light to shine.

Facing trials oft times, my flesh grows so weak.
Teach me to in thee be strong.
For the course is very rugged, Lord, and the mountains run steep;
Yet hope rest in Your arms.

Oh, free me, Dear Lord, from the briars of my vessel,
And help me come forth as pure gold.
Your tests are honorable and lead to a reality of truth
That can not be bought or sold.

Great is Your faithfulness, Your words in me dwell.
Convict me not to bring reproach to Your name.
Magnify the blessed light that abides from within,
So your words I will boldly proclaim.

Though I fall short of the glory on this side of Heaven,
I'll never walk alone without Thee.
For I know in the Earth and Heaven above,
There is none as faithful as He!

PASSION VERSES: I COR. 10:13, ROM. 3: 23-
26; 7:21-25, PS. 89:1-8 & LAM. 3:22-23

"THAT SINFUL ESTATE"

You're aching with pain, but yet you hurt others.
Never confronting yourself, you blame another.
You won't embrace God's peace, so you wage war instead.
Becoming spiritually deadened by your very own hand.

Comforting your conscience is what you do best,
Because the shackles of rebellion are bound at your neck!
Preoccupied with you, and only pleasing yourself;
The unmet needs of others, you continually reject.

Lacking remorse in your heart, you leave souls on a limb,
Hoping their fall will shadow your horrid guilt within.
O, you're living sin…you just won't admit it.
Drifting into darkness and drawn to like spirits.

Is where you find yourself part of your purposed plight?
Does God want you living on the edge of the night?
The answer is quite simple; yes; there is a way of escape.
But it's found only in Jesus; what a price He has paid!

He seeks you His servant, and sees you afar off.
Yes, a fatted calf awaits and a precious white robe.
Just come to the Master; there's no need to wait.
No, you don't have to live in that sinful estate!

PASSION VERSES: JER. 3: 20-22, HOS.14 & LK. 15: 11-24

"ANCHORED THE LIGHT"

In the morning when you rise,
Surviving the perils of the night;
Thank the true God of Heaven,
That you're anchored in the light.

You are a beautiful ship of Zion
That will voyage many great seas.
The helm is in His hands,
As He's mapped your destiny.

He will speak peace upon the waters.
He will command joy to be displayed,
And Heaven will bow its goodness
As you journey through your day.

The darkness will not rule you,
For He is a consuming fire.
All brightness abides around Him,
At no escape of His desire!

Yes, many violent storms will come,
And even raging waves may rise;
Yet your course will not be broken,
For your are anchored in the Light!

PASSION VERSES: HEB. 6:17-20, PS. 91: 1-5; 46:1-5 & 93

"DARK SHADOWS"

Dark shadows cross our room at night,
And to us they bring a shiver of fear.
Swift and silent as the raven's flight;
These things we can not see or hear.

They hide in the corner of our room.
We say to them, "Come closer.... draw near."
Not knowing they come to bring us gloom;
These things we can not see or hear.

They are things out of our lingering past.
We feel them here; and oh, so very near.
Phantoms for this life to last;
These things we can not see or hear.

Yet peace and solitude in Jesus we find,
As He erases shadows of memories not so dear.
The rooms in which they cross is our mind;
These things we can not see or hear.

PASSION VERSES: ROM. 12: 1-2, PHIL. 3: 13-16 & IS. 26: 3-4

"STRANGER NAMED LOVE"

"Pause stranger and abide with me.
Let my humble house be yours to command.
You are tired and hungry; I can well see,
And this dinner was prepared by my own good hands."

"Tell me of yourself, for this I wish to know;
Of how you happened upon this place…
Of people you have seen and know…,
And of the men who bowed to your charming grace."

With a face as bright as the moonlit sky,
While on my humble food He fed;
There was a twinkle in the stranger's eye,
As He smiled and thusly said…,

"I have traveled the world countless times around.
I have dwelled with people much like you.
Upon every heart I am to be found.
Out of sincere passion and desire I grew."

"I have been with kings and fools as well.
Yet to all, I am not a lasting friend.
I am swung in some hearts as a golden bell,
And will be with thee until the end."

"But stranger these things I do not understand,
For they are too difficult for my mind to see.
Your words are like a riddle told by Pan,
But tell me more, I beg of thee."

"My friend, I have talked long and now must go;
To float on the wind as a turtle dove.
But My name I leave for you always to know;
Thou men call me stranger, my name...is Love."

PASSION VERSES: I COR. 13:8; 13, ROM. 13:10 & I JN. 4:7-11

"GOING HOME"

Going home, going home...
No need to worry for me.
My coronation day has come;
And my crowning is sure and sweet.

Going home, going home...
Can you see it with my eyes?
The glory of His holiness,
And the thunder of the cries.

The many host of Heaven;
Singing praises to His name.
The sweet name of Jesus,
We continually proclaim.

I have gone home, family,
Turned in my borrowed tomb.
And this wonderful place in Jesus
Awaits your coming soon.

PASSION VERSES: PS. 116:15 & II TIM. 4: 6-8

"THEY'RE COMING IN"

They're coming in, they're coming in!
Saints of the most high God make way.
From the depths of the Earth and four corners within,
The sheaves that were once gone astray.

O, shepherds, be ye sober.
Take out your holy rods and sit upon the hill.
From the mount of the Lord you shall see them.
They're coming in, they're coming in!

They have heard the Master calling.
Feed them from pastures a'green.
For now is the time they are hungry.
Glory to God, what an awesome scene!

They're coming in from everywhere,
Nations and tongue from every clan and tribe;
To the vineyard of our Holy One.
They're coming in, they're coming in,
Yes, the hour has come!

PASSION VERSES: EZ. 34: 1-12, REV. 7:1-3; 9-12 & JER. 23:1-4

"FOREVER AND ALWAYS FRIENDS"

Friends are for always,
For true ones are seldom found.
Their support and comfort will find you
When you are up or down.

Forever and always friends,
Seeking to understand the real you.
They may not agree with your every word,
But will respect your point of view.

Yes, friends are forever.
Thank God for this wonderful gift.
For you have given friendship precious meaning;
Forever and always friends.

PASSION VERSES: PROV. 27: 6,9 & JN. 15: 13-15

"FRIENDSHIP"

We should always take the time to say
Exactly how we truly feel.
Yet sometimes we forget to mention to friends
Just why they are held so dear.

Friendship is not an easy thing,
Yet many hold this faulty view.
It takes patience, hard work, and lots of love
For pure friendships to endure.

So, I just thought I'd take a few moments to say,
Thanks for being such a good friend.
May our friendship weather the test of time
And meet its rewarding end.

PASSION VERSES: PROV. 17:17; 27:17 & 18:24

"THANKS, GOD"

For every blessing that meets my eye,
And for every tear drop from lessons I cry;
I triumphantly smile and nod…
"Thanks, God!"

Though much of the time I do not understand;
Yea; understand the reasoning and wicked state of man.
How great is Thy comforting rod…
So I pause to say, "Thank you, God!"

Unsure of what tomorrow may bring;
Wondering if caged will I ever sing.
As in season when a pea pops from its pod…
My soul, too, ripens and states, "Thanks, God!"

Thank you for all of the gifts you have given.
From the lessons learned, my soul was driven;
To boldly follow Thee, walking by unspeakable faith.
No, not granting uncertainty the time to wreck my pace.

For one never can earn all that you have done.
Behold, the blessed giving of your only begotten Son!
So in our greatest effort, we feebly stand to applaud;
For all of your love, joy and peace…
"Thanks, God!"

PASSION VERSES: PS. 68: 18-19, EPH. 5:20 & 1: 3-4

"THE BOW AND ARROWS OF HATE"

They cut as knives, the arrows of hate;
Bowing at its victims, much chaos they create.

The jagged edges once pierced lead to total destruction.
Walking in nigh target, one bleeds from their touches.

Aiming at the foot of man, driving him to fallow ground;
Lurking in the shadows of life are these arrows found.

Embedded in unrighteousness lives the horrid bower.
he joyously sharpens each fatal blade over and over.

Oh; but there does lie a secret place of hiding,
And for those who seek shelter, a home is provided.

There lives no principality or power that can shake His Holy State.
No, not even the dreaded bow and arrows of hate.

PASSION VERSES: JN. 5:18-21, PS. 18: 14-
18; 57: 4-6; 91: 1-16 & COL. 2:9-10

"STEADFAST AWHILE"

Steadfast awhile, I plead to all.
You must live righteously and wait.
Be ye perfect and stand without blemish, God says,
Before the time is too late!

It is not complex as most make it seem.
satan eludes them with his practice.
he is a deceiver I know, and the father of lies;
Yet greater is He in us than his tactics!

Yielding to the flesh and living to this life
Reaps no reward, pay or salvation.
So, rebuke the chains that entangle you,
And seek God through all deed, thought and action.

Hark, the time is at hand when the Savior shall appear,
Removing all who themselves defile.
So, press on in the Name of Jesus, I beg;
For we must steadfast awhile.

PASSION VERSES: EPH. 6:10-18, I JN.4:4 & I COR.15: 57-58

"JUST LIKE THE EAGLE"

I will rest in Jesus; my portion is Him.
Just like the eagle, I'll soar to the end.

Nothing will beset me; I will drink from my cup.
Just like the eagle, on wings I'll mount up.

My strength He'll renew; I will live and not die.
Just like the eagle, I'll conquer the sky!

Over the storms I'll fly, reaching my mark.
Then like the eagle, I too, will embark.

Embark on the mountain, that holy height above.
Just like the eagle, I will rest in God's love.

PASSION VERSES: IS. 40: 30-31 & 2: 2-3

"DAUGHTER OF JERUSALEM"

"You are a pearl; yes, a precious jewel.
I have fashioned you meet for My use;
To pour out My love to others you meet,
My faithful and steadfast tool.

Yes, I see those sparrows in your backyard.
That bed is truly their resting place;
And just like that home satisfies their needs,
Yours too, my love, I'll embrace.

Your season is nigh; you will tarry not long,
As I am preparing for your departure.
Your ship of Zion will anchor in waters,
Running deep to comfort the sorrows;

The sorrows of my little, my little sheep,
The ones who have drifted away.
Daughter of Jerusalem, steer them back.
Now rest in My words, I say."

PASSION VERSES: HAB. 2:3, ECCL. 3: 1,11 & PS. 119:73

"I'M DEPENDING ON YOU"

I look to you Father; Author and Finisher of my faith.
Oh, how my eyes are fixed upon Thee!
Just to please You, Master; my Hope of all glory,
Your commandments I hunger to keep.

Oh Lord, my God; Great Shepherd of my soul,
I beckon you to hear my anguishing cry.
Lamenting from the core of my innermost being,
I long only for Your touch from on high.

The things I desire not to do,
My flesh cries out to fulfill.
What a battle is it sweet Jesus, my Love
To believe in patience and be still!

Yet I know my anchor and strength lies in You.
Aid me in the stead-fasting of Your will.
I'm depending on You; Abba Father, my Friend
To kindle my fire again!

PASSION VERSES: HEB.12:2, ROM. 7:18-24 & 8:15-17

"WHOM SHALL I FEAR?"

As I breathe, walk and live in a world full of sin…
As I travel the tedious roads brimmed with deception and bends…
I take the time to ask myself,
"Whom shall I fear?"

When success tilts toward failure…
When friends forsake and are no longer familiar…
I stand still erect and say,
"Whom shall I fear?"

To feel there is a loss of light…
And cornered desperately, searching for a reason why…
My dear mother, my dear Father,
Whom shall I fear?"

I shall fear not a world, nor challenging roads thereof traveled,
Neither failure or a loss of friends.
To fear nothing and have peace when all seems to crumble,
Is to know the love of Jesus, our Savior within.

"Tell me then, whom shall I fear?
For the Lord is the Light of my salvation."

PASSION VERSE: PS. 27: 1-5

"JESUS LORD, OUR REDEEMER"

Jesus Lord, Our Redeemer; He who saved us from the bottomless pit of hell,
Upon His Rock, build your church; where hell's gates can not prevail.

He rules with an iron hand, and His mighty lessons you must heed.
He has taught us to rebuke the devourer…resist him and he will flee.

He is the God that suffers long, yet will He in no wise be mocked.
Kiss Him to kindle not His jealously, or His correction He will impart.

His laws are pure and righteous; they will always and forever stand.
Trust in His unsearchable ways, and forsake the arm of man.

Eschew evil and be a lover of truth to quench all fiery darts.
For today is the day of salvation; choose not to harden your hearts!

Jesus is the only Lord, saving those who completely surrender.
All praises be to the Most High God; Jesus Lord, our Redeemer!

PASSION VERSES: GAL.4:4-5, JAS. 4:7, PS. 19:7; 8:14 & JOB 19: 25

"A GRANDMOTHER"

What a joy it is to be called a grand!
Someone great and special; such a heart that mends.

What really makes a grandmother all that she is?
I have been curious to study that family trend.

Rising early in the morning to start off her day,
As she first meets with Jesus to show her the way.

The way to touch lives of her family and friends;
Never seeking any glory and never casting a blame.

She reaches in love everyone that she touches,
Changing heartbeats in destiny or aiding in minor adjustments.

You'll seldom see her cry, or be overwhelmed with sorrow.
For she understands the plan of God, as she faces each tomorrow.

I guess on my own, I have truly figured it out.
A grandmother is beyond words without a doubt.

Grandma, this grandmother we see is you;
A honored queen in our hearts and in the eyes of Heaven, too.

PASSION VERSE: II TIM. 1:5 & PROV. 31: 10-31

"A GREAT DAY"

It is a great day, Dear Lord...
A great day!
A day granted unto me to prosper or faint...
To walk or be weary, to discard or obtain...
The choice is left up to me!

It is a great day, Dear Lord...
Oh, what a day!
Leaving the decision in my hands...
To fail or succeed, to fall or stand...
The choice is left up to me!

What a day Your voice has brought into being.
The beauty it holds such color and meaning.
The trees bend at Your command,
And as directed the seas move across the lands.

Yet you extend to me free will...
To move or sit still...
The choice is left up to me!

It is a great day, Dear Lord, and my soul is rest assured.
Knowing I will search the paths You have set for me to endure.
Although it gets rough and quite trying at times,
You have bestowed unto me Your blessed peace of mind.

It is a great day…

It is a wonderful day…

Yes, another day that You, Dear Lord hath made!

PASSION VERSES: JOSH. 24:15, PS.19:1-4; & 118:24

"ROPES OF IRON"

Strand by strand, woven by Heaven above.
Appear ropes of iron, streamed from God;

Flowing down from the heights of His holy hill;
Solely destined their course toward the heart of man's will.

Elevating us over life's failures and pits,
Hearken ropes of iron for the children of men.

Embrace them; my son, and don't dare let go!
Long life they will bring and cancel all woe.

For in loosing those strings made of sin and sand,
We possess our liberty; ropes of iron from His hands.

PASSION VERSES: PROV. 3: 1-2; 4:5-10 & MT. 7:24-27

"WHO AM I?"

Who am I?
Do you really want to know?
Many inquiring minds have asked me.
I puzzle many I'm told.

You thought it was in my height,
The cubit of my stature.
Well, you've seen how I dress…
Do you think that will help you?

Or maybe it's where and how I live;
Certainly, that would give you a big clue…
Or perhaps the car I ride in
Could tell you a thing or two.

Who am I?
Do you really want to know?
The natural man can't figure me out,
But I'm not complicated, you know.

Are you watching my circle of friends?
Have you researched my family tree?
Do they tell you much
Or anything at all truly about me?

Am I my father's child?
No, no…my mother's son…

I could be my sister's brother
Or even a grandson…

Money…money, you say?
Do I have any?
Huh.. I'm sorry, my friend;
That answer won't help you either.

Who am I?
Hmm…I bet you wonder.
You must really want to know
To go through such trouble!

Well, I'll tell you…
I am a child of God,
Destined for the kingdom of Heaven.
Who I am is in my nature.
Who I am is in my character.

I am a person of love.
I am a person of peace.
With joy I face valleys low
And every mountain peak.

But I'm not perfect;
I do blow it sometimes.
But Jesus is there to pick me up,
And put me back in line.

Not in family or friends…
No, not in a home or a car…
Not even in your pocket, my friend,
Will you find who you are.

So, dig deep inside yourself.
Look into your spirit man,
And who you really are
Will echo loud from within.

Who am I?
Well, now you truly know.
To think the answer all the time was right beneath your nose.

PASSION VERSES: ROM. 8:16-17 & LK. 18: 16-17

"GIVE UNTO THE LORD"

Give unto the Lord, O, ye servants.
Give unto the Lord; bless His soul!
Give of your heart, substance, and time,
For the Lord is worthy of it all!

Laws of increase, follow laws of release,
So, open your hands up wide.
As you give unto Him, He'll return unto you
Great measure beyond your surprise!

PASSION VERSES: PS. 29:1-2, LK. 6:38 & MAL. 3:10-11

"TOO MUCH IS GIVEN"

God has given us too much to give so little back,
So dig deep into your heart today.
For the many talents and wholesome gifts,
We are called to share in grace.

Do not resume a life of toil
Or even the thought of a troublesome way.
For He is the Victor; therefore, are we.
So endeavor to seek Him always.

We've been given too much to give so little back.
Let's take the time to assess the need today.
Someone is waiting for your touch or smile
To help them along the way.

The anointing was given to meet the needs of the sheep;
To encourage hope and patience to stand.
God has given us too much to give so little back,
So, together let's meet the demand.

PASSION VERSES: I COR. 12:4-7, EPH. 4:1-
7, ROM. 12:4-6 & PS. 133:1-2

"HEAVEN AWAITS"

Praising our eternal Father through beautiful song…
Yes, singing and rejoicing the whole day long…
This is what Heaven holds for me!

Never a problem or trying time…
Nor worry or reason for dreadful crime…
Heaven awaits with this for you!

The streets of solid gold, I do plainly see…
As I listen when the elders tell stories unto me…
Heaven holds this for you!

No place allowed to trouble to hide…
Only a home to rest the weary mind…
One must believe that Heaven is true!

Our time passes rapidly; we must take a stand,
To believe now in God, clasping His Son's hand.
For if we trust that by Him, we are free,
Heaven awaits patiently for you and me!

PASSION VERSES: REV. 21:1-4, 18-26 & 19:4-6

"TO BE CALLED A SERVANT"

We seek to instruct, yet defy instruction.
We look to teach, yet refuse to be taught.
When will we grow; oh, when will we know,
That we must serve to be called a servant.

Seeking for a ministry, we forget to minister.
Looking for a hand-out, but seldom extending a hand.
When will we see; yea, when will we be,
One who serves to be called a servant.

We strive for a holy title, yet forsake its sole duty.
Reaching for power and authority, we sacrifice character.
When will we become those true sons of God,
And know we must serve to be called a servant.

If you are seeking to be great, great ones seek to serve.
If you are desiring a ministry, learn to live the Word.
For if your longing is conceived in true servitude,
Your joint will supply, and your joy shall be full.
Discovering Heaven's key you will be made free,
By being one who serves to be called a servant.

PASSION VERSES: MT. 23:1-33 & 20: 25-28

"ALL ANSWERS HE KNOWS"

What lies ahead for you and I,
Behind the dark corners of our lives?

What will each break of morning bring?
Who will give the answers to the things unseen?

When we are down, who will lift us high?
Who can dry the water from our tear-stained eyes?

Who will answer our call in the midnight hour?
Who will encourage us to fight on with enduring power?

As we share our triumphs, who is most happiest of all?
Who will give direction to avoid any great fall?

What must lie in a name for so much to be done?
Who can give the answers to everyone?

His name is Jesus; He is our Prince of Peace.
Only He can meet and supply all our needs.

What lies in His name is a blessed hope.
It is the name of Jesus, for all answers He knows.

PASSION VERSES: PS 146:3-5, ROM. 5:1-5 & JUDE 1:24-25

"GLAD TO BE ME"

Do you know how many people who are proud to be who they are?
Can you number how many are not ashamed of some
terrible childhood scar?

Some feel they never reached their career goals in life,
And allow themselves to suffer the guilt from the lack of trying.

Others seem a bit displeased with their spiritual or moral estate,
While many say there is no Heaven or hell and controversially debate.

I, personally, am so glad just to be me,
For by God's grace… from their worries, am I set truly free!

PASSION VERSES: PROV. 3:13-15, PS.128:1-2 & ROM. 8:36

"MY GREATEST LOVE STORY"

No tender touch could dare compare to the sweet, soft touch of the lamb.
He cradles me in His loving arms and saves me from the thicket of the ram.

As I lay my head upon His chest, an inner tranquility floods my soul.
His fragrant aroma, the smell of honey, doth my every sense behold.

Under His wings, so near and dear, He clothes me with an array of love,
And then He whispers with the voice of a harp,
His wonders and countless joys.

His tender mercies are ever before me, whether I forbear with Him or leave.
My cup runneth over, for I can not contain His fullness given to me.

My greatest love story, the best I have ever known,
have I experienced with Him.
And He wants to freely love all this way, if only we would let Him in.

He should be no stranger to any man;
a marriage covenant He desires to extend.
Such faithfulness and unconditional love
He has purposed in His heart to give.

Therefore, my tongue to my day of rest will lift Him in honor,
admiration and praise.
Jesus, Jesus, the love of my life, I exalt your wonderful and holy name!

PASSION VERSES: SONG 1:1-4; 12-17; 3:1-
4, PROV. 15:17, JN. 15:13 & 3:16

"WILL YOU RECEIVE HIM?"

Look to Him who can fasten your feet,
And keep you from all ploys of evil.
Trust in Him who has no dark region,
Yielding pure righteousness in all season.

Believe in Him who died to redeem,
Who for the joy set before Him did endure.
Hope in Him with a patience unceasing,
Laying to heart the purity of His Word.

Abide in His mercy, and hide thy face in His bosom,
Leave no occasion of stumbling
Love Him with all thy heart, strength and mind,
And await the brightness of His coming.

For now is the time to know that you know
The destiny and the Inheritor of your soul.
Lest a tomorrow awaits, marred with perpetual pain
In which you will have no control.

Will you receive Him in spirit and truth
To deliver your soul from eternal damnation?
Jesus is the answer, as no other name will save,
And He alone gives everlasting salvation.

PASSION VERSES: ROM.10:9-11, REV.3:20, ST. JN.10:9 & 3:5-7

"THERE IS STILL MUCH WORK TO BE DONE"

O, how we long to see the new Heaven,
The revelation of glory revealed through God.
Yet on this side of Jordon, we run this great travel.
And there is still much work to be done.

On to perfection, we must press toward the mark,
The holy tabernacle of God to come.
We must focus on building His kingdom on Earth.
Yes, there is still much work to be done.

Know that he that endures, shall inherit the promise.
We will be His sons, and He our God.
Not a minute to waste, nor waiver or complain;
There's just too much work to be done.

Now be of good courage for just this little while,
As His great work in you has begun.
He shall finish your faith, and our season shall come,
Yet now there is much work to be done!

PASSION VERSES: JN. 9:4, MT. 9: 36-
38, I COR. 3:6-9 & PHIL. 3:14-15

"TIME VERSES SLOTH"

A rapid wind blows me,
As I hear the tires screech…
Breaking my stride and racing heart,
Another bus has passed me by!

The frustration on my face…
A crumbled transfer in my hand…
Couldn't the driver see me?
But he chose to go on instead.

Taking a long breath,
I threw back my head and sat…
As I blamed that crazy driver;
He could have given me break!

Come…come…; Hurry…hurry…
They eagerly steal the course of my days.
How does this mad rush anticipate me?
There must be a more excellent way.

Then echoing out of nothingness,
There was an audible voice in the air.
And as I turned toward its direction,
It grew louder for me to hear.

It said, "Time verses Sloth".
If you lose, nothing is gained.
No, not the driver, my child;
It is time that waits for no man."

I shook, and I trembled…
Yet it wasn't from below…
As the voice began to fade,
With the earthquake in my soul.

What a challenge of priority;
Such an enlightenment of truth.
Truly sharper than a two-edged sword,
I must change my attitude.

So, looking toward the Heavens…
As humbly as I knew…
Fighting back the tears,
I gently whispered…
Lord, help me to catch…
I mean…teach me to wait for the next one.

PASSION VERSES: PROV. 18:19, ECCL.
10:18, HEB. 6:11-12 & PROV. 13:4

"THE OLD FOLKS USED TO SAY"

"Trouble don't last always…they'll be a brighter day…"
That's what the ole' folks used to say.

"You keep yo' chin up, child…no time to grow weary, nor tire…
Justa' cause the color yo' skin, you gonna' quit and give in,

We's a'free, child!
This day, we's a free!

Can't no chain shackle yo' mind…
Prejudice can't hold you down on every side…
We done come a long way, and many men done shed blood.
Many battles done been fought, and still some victories to be won.

But we's a'free, child!
This day, we's a'free!"

The old folks were 'buked, and terribly scorn.
Ripped from the love of families… battered, broken and worn.
Yet God understood their struggles, weariness and pain.
As I sit and meditate on what the ole' folks use to say.

And there's still racial barriers we must face as a people.
And among the blessed strong, there will always be the feeble.
Is the real enemy and threat truly mankind?
Or does the ugly beast exist within our human mind?

These are the things I've questioned.
The heart of asperity and assumption.

And as the hand of time continually turns on.
Decades roll by, and a new millennium has come.

It's only when I feel that I can't go on no more.
I figure I'm just passing through life's open door.
"Trouble don't last always...they'll be a brighter day..."
That's what I've learned to say.

PASSION VERSE: II COR. 4: 8-18

"The Love of Jesus"

The precious love of Jesus surrounds my soul.
A love so great, it alone I can't hold.

If He only gave every blessing to me,
My cup would spill over, and I'd make my own sea!

That is why His love from Heaven He just sprinkles,
For every man to fly high upon just as the eagle.

A perfect love it is, that shines brilliant and bright,
For He loves us when we're wrong, and loves us when we're right.

In few words, I guess one could easily say;
It is the love of Jesus that grant us hope today.

Passion Verses: Rom. 5:8; 8:35-39 & I Jn. 3:1

"MY SAVIOR LIVES"

The stone has been rolled away.
My savior lives; He has conquered the grave!

O, grave, where is your victory?
O, heart of death, where is your sting?

The Lamb has taken the key.
The kingdom of Christ has come, and your spoiled unleashed.

Now my sins are all washed away,
And by His precious blood, I am cleansed today.

PASSION VERSES: JN. 20:1-9, I COR. 15: 53-57, REV. 1: 17-18 & HEB. 9: 12-14

"A GREATER GLORY"

From faith to faith, then glory to glory, the Master is calling unto you.
Yes, your faith will embark a new frontier of glory living assure.

At the omega of this blessed trail, a greater capacity expands in you.
It may not yet appear, but new doors He's bringing you through.

He has seen your faith, O shepherd and has imputed righteousness;
Strengthening thy stakes, lengthening thy cords,
and enlarging the place of thy tent.

So, continue to stand son of Zion, fully clothed in the garment of praise.
For greener pasture He has promised; yea; a greater glory awaits.

PASSION VERSES: HEB.11:1, ROM. 1:16-17, JAS. 2:23 & HAG. 2:9

"HOLY WORLD WITHOUT END"

Everlasting to everlasting, holy world without end,
All Heaven unfolds unto the children of men!

No wicked order shall stand to rule or reign.
No false sense of peace will His government proclaim.

All sinful systems will be brought to naught.
By the testimony of His tongue, they will lie in default.

Only love, victory and peace will this new world follow,
As heavenly over comers awake to this blessed morrow.

Confessed by every tongue, Jesus shall reign forever as King,
As the saints possessed the inheritance; holy world without end!

PASSION VERSES: REV. 21;1, 3:12, ROM.
14:11, EPH. 1:11-14 & IS. 45:17-18

"O, WORTHY POTTER"

Keep us in your joy, I pray;
An attitude of thanksgiving and praise.

Cultivate humility, grace and truth.
Extend your love and tender mercies, too.

Shape our lives, O, Worthy Potter.
Complete this work of glory and honor.

Round and round upon Your will,
As you make us more like You within.

And when You press, we will dare not wrestle;
Considering only the finished vessel.

O, Worthy Potter, you see it all;
Our past, our present and what we shall become.

PASSION VERSES: JER. 18: 1-6, MAL. 3:3,
PROV. 17:3, HEB. 12:2 & PHIL. 1:6

"ARISE"

I was sinking fast.
Didn't think I would last,
But I will arise…

For my wounds did stink,
Because of my foolishness;
But I will arise…

Though my enemies hath tried
To snare my very life,
I will arise…

Back to my Father's house…
Back to my loving Spouse…
I will arise…

Completely forgiven and free…
Walking in total victory…
I will arise…

To leave no more…
His loving arms…
I will arise…

Though a just man falls seven times,
He will arise…

I will arise…I will arise…
Hallelujah to God; I will arise!

PASSION VERSES: PS. 51 & PROV. 24:16

Prelude to Love

One of the most misunderstood, misrepresented and perverted human emotions of all time is often guised as the "*heart of love.*" Over many years, my personal definition of love has been painstakingly challenged and completely transformed during my close walk and journey with the Lord. I have come to learn that we as human beings, so easily embrace some very challenging, compromised and dysfunctional images as it relates to true love and its genuine expressions. We so often stake claims in love that are driven by immaturity, pretense, selfish gain, lust and immorality. All of which are very far from the essence of love as defined by God in light of the Holy Scriptures (I Cor. 13).

To know true love is to know the Father, for the Gospel in one word is "Love" (I Jn. 4: 7-21). God commands us to love; it is more than a mere life suggestion or option. *In the Old Testament God speaks through Moses,* His chosen spiritual leader and summons him to deliver a command to His people in Deut. 6: 4-5. Moses thus announces, "Hear, O Israel: The Lord our God is one Lord, and thou shalt love the Lord thy God with all thy heart, and with all thy soul, and with all thy might." It is apparent God makes this announcement at a very critical time of transition in Israel's history, to also state if they can be true and pure in their love for Him; there is no level of covenant relationship they will not fully come to know, embrace and honor. *In the New Testament, God speaks through His Son, Jesus* and states the essentialness of life through a new command, instructing us to love our neighbor as ourselves (Mk. 12:29-31).

Upon these two greatest commandments hang the entire law (Ex. 20:
1-17; Mt. 22:37-40). They are both commands that are founded and
established in unfeigned love and uncompromised reverence for the
Father and humanity, which inevitably compels us to love in both word
and deed on all levels and platforms of life. In honoring the first com-
mand to Love God with all, we embrace the first five of the ten com-
mandments; as they are directly tied to our eternal relationship and
covenant with Him. In honoring the second command towards love
for our neighbor, we embrace the last five commandments, as they
are directly tied to our relationships and covenants with all of man-
kind. Therefore, if we truly love God we will keep his commandments
(Jn.14:15), and if we keep His commandments, we abide in His love
and joy (Jn. 15: 10-11). God in turn, keeps *His covenant* and mercy to
them that love Him and keep His commandments to a thousand gen-
erations (Deut. 7:9).

When any covenant relationship whether it be marriage, family, work,
friendship or otherwise is absent of God's love, issues of the heart most
naturally and progressively take an extreme and drastic turn for the
worse. Images, thoughts and feelings of dishonor and disrespect quick-
ly fester and manifest into despicable behavior and unbearable pain in
relationships. The impact is devastating. On the contrary, a true love
walk that is fervent and embedded in God's love has the capacity, if we
allow it, to keep and govern our relationships in even the most difficult
of times, especially with those who are considered to be unlovable or
those who would otherwise be regarded as enemies (Mt. 5:43-48).

Living a life of love does not demand we be a "door mat" for others.
It just simply means we daily crucify our ill-motives in our response
and actions toward others, even in the face of betrayal, persecution or
suffering. Love calls us to commit and completely surrender all of our
affairs to the leading and guiding of the Holy Spirit. Imagine what a
world it would be if every relationship and interaction was governed by
tailor-made love actions designed solely by God!

"*Agape*" is the Greek word for "*love*." It is a love that is sacrificial and unconditional in nature (Jn. 3:16-17). The faulty view, misconception and erroneous teaching of agape misleads us to believe God is accepting of a lifestyle of sin. God forbid. The real truth is, once we accept Jesus Christ as our Lord and personal Savior and give our hearts and lives over to Him, God's love rescues us! His love is so far-reaching, that no matter how dark or sinful our lives are, His love is greater than the darkness and the sin. His true love changes us for the better (Ps. 139:7-18; I Jn. 3:20)

"Agape" is always motivated to give, yet lust desires to take, abuse and misuse at every opportunity. The evil state of our world can be directly linked to the ill and misplaced love of many. As a result, our love has waxed so cold! (Mt. 24:12). Our world is now paying the cost of our greed, love for money, lust for power and authority (I Ti. 6:6-10).

However, the remedy is quite simple. A great song writer once said, "What the world needs now is love, sweet love". It truly is the only thing that there is much too little of in this world. The manifestation of love is the heart cry of mankind! God gave us the perfect example through the sacrificing of His Son. No man took His life, but He laid it down that we may live. He came not to be ministered to, but to minister life to all (Mk. 10:45). If we deliberately strive to love each other to the degree that God has so loved us, we too will lay down our lives for each other. For there is no greater love! (Jn. 15:12-13)

scriptural references for the following poems are covered in the prelude
"FOREVER KEEPSAKE"

Day by day, many come and go;
Passing through the corridors in our lives.
The joy of love and laughter is shared ,
Then awaits many sad goodbyes.

Crossing in and out the lives of others,
Leaving trails of goodness behind,
Hoping these trails of kindness to see,
Will some cherish deep inside.

Astonishing it is, the direction God leads,
Many paths in life to do.
Just when you feel you meet a fork in the road,
He sends someone to help you through.

I am compelled to say, our feelings are real,
And they mean so much to me.
Although some come, although some go,
You have stayed around to see;

The radiant vision of our heart and lives,
Truly a blessing send from above.
Helping hand as we share this life,
I give freely and openly in love.

I have looked long and wide, being careful to see.
Few love, but many hate.
Yet the gift of love God has given to use
Will remain forever keepsake.

"SISTERHOOD IN CHRIST"

Whom shall I call my sister?
Whom shall I call my friend?
The answer Jesus gives in His Word
Speaks expressly unto this end.

Is she one with whom I share secrets,
Or maybe she just frequently calls?
Does she refresh me when I'm weary,
Reaching to lift me when I fall?

Does my success truly make her happy,
Rejoicing and commemorating my honor.
Does she hurt when I face failure,
Choosing to bear my grief and sorrow?

Yes, she is one who builds me up.
No, she'll never let me down.
Upon her lips rest counsel and wisdom,
And her compassion is sure and sound.

She is strong, yet meek;
Solely pursuing the course of truth.
Her wounds have been found faithful.
She is humble, embracing correction and reproof.

She will love me at all times,
Looking beyond my human error.
The sacred view of God is seen
In the image that she mirrors.

Steadfast in God's command;
She is my sister, indeed.
For we share a unique blood line,
Bonded by a common heartbeat.

Oh, whom shall I call my sister?
Tell me, whom shall I call my friend?
Yes, your portrait of this meaning
Speaks expressly to this end.

"IN GOD LIES OUR STRENGTH"

A sharing this precious; O, so rare,
I am convinced God ordained from above.
Let us be strong in the direction it will lead,
Knowing in God lies our strength and our love.

This sacred sharing is merely a shadow type
Of our holy union and covenant with God.
Our destiny and hope is in His hands,
For in God lies our strength and our love.

"HUSBANDS AND WIVES"

Husbands and wives, striving to be one flesh;
An unending challenge with very little rest.

Sacrifice, sacrifice, we're told over and over again.
When will unity rise and the chaos end!

When will our men stand as head of the home?
When will they take responsibility for what they condone?

And wives, Oh, women, when will you learn to submit,
And not throw in the towel, lie down or quit?

Are we as couples sincerely praying enough?
Are we humbling ourselves, although it be tough?

God said there would be some trouble in the flesh,
And how right He was, I must confess.

So, let's not bow down; we are the head and not the tale.
For God is completely able; through Him we shall prevail.

He is touched by our heartache, infirmities and fear.
Do we really trust in trouble His grace is ever so near?

It is imperative that we hold on to the biblical truths,
Living a covenantal lie just will not do.

Then husbands and wives shall become of one flesh,
And though the growing pains continue, in Jesus we rest.

PASSION VERSES: I COR. 7:3 & EPH. 5:21-25

"YOUR LOVE FOR ME"

Now I know your love for me, for I see it through God's eyes.
It was difficult for me to see, searching through the natural mind.

Now I hear you love for me when I listen to your voice.
I couldn't hear before, because I wouldn't make the choice.

Now I feel your love for me in view of God's Holy Word.
Before I allowed the emotional realm to make my heart quite numb.

Now I smell a sweet savor; the aroma of sacrifice,
Knowing that your love for me has reached a blessed height.

"TAKE MY HAND AND SHARE IN MY WORLD"

The happiness you have brought into my life
In such a short, yet precious moment of time,
Has awakened my heart and opened the door
To shadowed feelings, longing freedom inside.

Your smile, your touch and ever pleasant way,
Gives my life a great sense of joy.
You have extended to me the temper of balance
Through a strong and genuine character as yours.

God saw it worthy and pleasing in His sight
To lead our varying paths to cross.
A taste of His love, He has given to us;
Oh, I love how it freely flows!

I have learned to understand the words in your eyes;
Hearing much of what is too difficult to speak.
I'm learning to cherish the tenderness shared,
As our hearts so gently meet.

I pray our marriage will continually grow,
And by the grace of God may we live.
Take my hand and share in my world.
You will find I have much love to give.

"WILL YOU STILL?"

Will you still love me when I'm old and gray?
Will you still hold me when trouble comes our way?

Will you still kiss my lips on days when they aren't colored?
Or will you yield your lips to meet the bosom of another?

Will you still walk with me when it seems all trust is gone?
Will you still pray with me when everything seems wrong?

Will you still remember our special wedding day?
Or will this be a distant thought you choose to tuck away?

Will you still stand by me and love me as your wife?
Or will you seek to close me out the essence of your life?

I am sure there are thousands of questions asking, "Will you still?"
Yet in my heart, I have answered them all, ending with, "I will."

"I'LL ALWAYS LOVE YOU"

Though the tides of life may come our way,
When mountain-top victories seem so far away;
Please know that I'll always love you…

When the rocky roads face our paths,
And when shattered dreams tumble fast;
Just know that I'll always love you…

In times that our laughter may fade to tears,
When it seems like the end of hope is near;
In these times, I choose to always love you…

No matter what hazard satan may try to bring,
As the robin we must learn to always sing.
And if this song of hope and faith abides,
God will see us through these trying times.
Just remember…I will always love you.

"BE WILLING TO WAIT"

More than a card or flower in happy or bad times.
Love means so very much more in my eyes.

More than a mate to help make ends meet,
Love rings a louder purpose to me.

Love is not selfish; no, it never seeks its own,
But it's always esteeming the other involved.

Chilling insensitivity is unknown to its course,
And cruelty and pride is not its driving force.

Love will sacrifice, opening its arms up wide
To caressingly receive you no matter the tide.

Fooled by its so-called faces, some are snared in a frame.
A frame with a black picture, possessing the shame;

The shame of impatience, the inability to wait,
Until God grooms and shapes, then reveals your mate.

We must listen and heed the call of the Holy Ghost,
And dare not step out without His support.

Then we will walk into marriage and not bite the wrong bait,
If we trust only in Jesus and be willing to wait.

"TOGETHER IN LOVE"

We share together in love…
A giving and receiving of exquisite intimacy,
Epitomized confidences and fears,
And even the smallest of joys.

We share together in love…
The exceptional individuality of each other in true spirit and heart,
Love that expels the tender, yet passionate feelings
That words so inadequately express.

We share together in love…
The essence of an idealistic romance,
That exist only for many in dreams;
A joyously reality of hope, happiness, and consolation.

So, let us walk the demanding, yet righteous walk
That few dare to travel to meet the brilliant end of love.
Let us freely commit to give our all
To share together in love.

"TRUE LOVE"

I have finally discovered the true meaning of love.
It is not found in the physical.
It is beyond the mystical.
It confounds the realm of sensible.
The true meaning of love…

I am experiencing true love at the heart of its core.
It is not empty or vain;
Nor based on wealth or fame.
It is a reflection of honor which holds no shame.
The true meaning of love…

The true essence of love, I am now able to give.
I have come to see the difference,
By learning to love for the distance.
Yes, through long-suffering and forbearance
Lies the true meaning of love.

Doors that were once closed, true love has now opened.
I see not only a lover,
But my friend and my brother.
Thus, I desire no other,
To share this early glimpse of true love…

Book Resources

Shakespeare and the History Of Soliloquies, (Fairleigh Dickinson Univ.)
Copyright 2006

Life Application Study Bible, King James Version
(Tyndale House Publishers, Inc.) Copyright 2004

Holy Bible, King James Version / Amplified Bible Parallel Edition
(Zondervan) Copyright 1995

Webster's Dictionary, Landoll, Inc. Copyright 1993

The New Unger Bible Dictionary, Merrill F. Unger (Moody Press Chicago)
Original Copyright 1957 / Revise & Updated Edition 1988

Printed in the USA
CPSIA information can be obtained
at www.ICGtesting.com
JSHW012043140824
68134JS00033B/3225